Incredibly Disgusting
Drugs™

W9-BCK-117

Marijuana

Jeanne Nagle

rosen publishing's
rosen
central®

New York

For Todd, because he couldn't wait to read this book

Published in 2008 by The Rosen Publishing Group, Inc.
29 East 21st Street, New York, NY 10010

Library of Congress Cataloging-in-Publication Data

Nagle, Jeanne M.
Marijuana / Jeanne Nagle.—1st ed.
    p.cm.—(Incredibly disgusting drugs)
Includes bibliographical references and index.
ISBN-13: 978-1-4042-1374-6 (library binding)
1. Marijuana. 2. Marijuana abuse. 3. Marijuana—Physiological effect. I. Title.
HV5822.M3N338 2008
613.8'35—dc22
                                        2007029650

Manufactured in the United States of America

Contents

Introduction

Talk to kids who do drugs and you might hear good things about marijuana. It's harmless, they say. They might talk about how good it makes them feel, or that smoking pot lets them forget about their problems for a while. Perhaps they claim that marijuana is "natural" and not considered a hard drug, so it really isn't bad for you. But the fact is there are plenty of negative consequences to smoking marijuana. For instance, let's take the flipside of the claim that "It feels good." The good feeling that users get is actually a sign that their brain cells are being damaged! And, sure, marijuana may be a natural substance, but so is tobacco. Just as with cigarettes, all that supposedly "organic" smoke still coats your lungs with gunk, making it difficult for you to breathe.

Another thing that users don't talk about much is that your entire being is subject to the awful effects of

Some users claim that smoking a little marijuana is a harmless way to relax. This attitude ignores all of the terrible damage it can do to your mind, body, and reputation.

marijuana. Your brain, your internal organs, and even your personality suffer every time you consume the stuff. You probably won't hear users talk about the fact that continuing to smoke marijuana makes it harder to stop. That's right: the more you smoke it, the more you crave the high marijuana gives. This high can make you so out of it that you completely ignore all the warning signs that your intelligence is being dulled and your health is suffering.

Smoking marijuana makes you forgetful, stains and rots your teeth, raises your risk of having a heart attack as you get older, and may make you unable to have children. It can rob you of your coordination, your looks, your ability to think clearly, and the will to make something of your life.

Now, does marijuana sound like a harmless drug to you?

The Facts About Marijuana

When you go up against something that is trying to hurt you, it helps to know a bit about it. That way, you are aware of your enemy's strengths and you can prepare to deal with them. This chapter gives you the lowdown on marijuana, so you'll understand the type of trouble you're up against if you decide to you use it.

A Little Background

Marijuana is the most commonly abused illegal drug in the United States. A 2005 survey indicates that 97 million Americans have at least tried pot, and 14.5 million are regular users. According to the National Institute on Drug Abuse, around 3.1 million Americans who are at least twelve years old use marijuana nearly every day. In both the United States and Canada, studies show that teens who use marijuana first tried it at fourteen years of age, on average.

Marijuana plants *(Cannabis sativa)* can be identified by their distinctive leaves. Growing marijuana is illegal in the United States.

Marijuana goes by many aliases, or names. These aliases include "pot," "weed," "dope," "grass," "bud," "herb," "ganja," "mary jane," and "cannabis." The drug grows as a plant called *Cannabis sativa*, which is a member of the hemp family. Hemp is legally grown in Europe, Asia, and Canada. Non-drug uses for the hemp plant include manufacturing clothing and rope from its fibers. It is also added to food as a supplement, and the plant's seeds can be pressed to make oil for paint and face creams.

The hemp plants used for industrial purposes are quite different from those grown for smoking. Industrial hemp plants have low levels of delta-9-tetrahydrocannabinol, or THC, which is the main drug-related chemical in marijuana. THC is a psychoactive substance, meaning it changes your mood and the way you think. Other psychoactive drugs include alcohol, amphetamines, ecstasy, cocaine, and heroin. They act on your central nervous system, altering the way your brain works by changing your

Marijuana smokers often roll dried leaves and buds of the *Cannabis sativa* plant in special papers. Smoking is the most common way to use marijuana.

perception, or your ability to become aware of and understand thoughts and actions. Psychoactive drugs also change your mood and how you act. Those who use marijuana say it makes them happier and better able to relax.

Because of its special properties, marijuana is also used as a medicine. Before it was declared illegal in the United States in the early 1900s, marijuana was used regularly as an ingredient in many prescription drugs—usually pain relievers—sold in this country. Today, just twelve U.S. states allow doctors to prescribe marijuana for medical treatment. When traditional drugs fail, smoking marijuana can help patients deal with extreme nausea or pain. The effects of marijuana also can help some patients cope with the awful pain associated with glaucoma (an eye disease) and multiple sclerosis. Despite these benefits, the federal government classifies marijuana as a drug that has a high potential for abuse and addiction and no medicinal value.

Brain Chemistry

In addition to a bunch of grey matter, your brain contains neurons, which are nerve cells that oversee all the information and activity in your brain. Neurons rely on chemicals called neurotransmitters, which the brain produces naturally. Neurotransmitters let neurons "talk" to each other. These chemicals send messages to receptors, the parts of your brain's nerve cells that control the actions of your body. Depending on the situation, receptors also can determine how you feel—happy or sad, calm or upset.

The brain has a special pathway called the pleasure circuit. Along this circuit, neurotransmitters send messages to neuron receptors, resulting in good feelings. The main natural "feel-good" chemicals at work within this pathway are dopamine and serotonin. Scientists recently discovered that the human brain also makes a pleasure neurotransmitter called anandamide. This chemical is classified as a cannabinoid neurotransmitter. This means it sends messages to the brain's receptors that are sensitive to chemicals found in *Cannabis sativa*—the marijuana plant.

Cannabinoid receptors are thickly concentrated in different parts of the brain. They are found in the cerebellum, which controls the body's movement and coordination. They are also found in the basal ganglia, which controls emotions and learning, and in the cerebral cortex, which is the part of the brain that controls logic and conversation. Cannabinoid receptors are also in the hippocampus, the part of the brain that controls memory. Not surprisingly, these are the same areas of the brain affected by smoking marijuana.

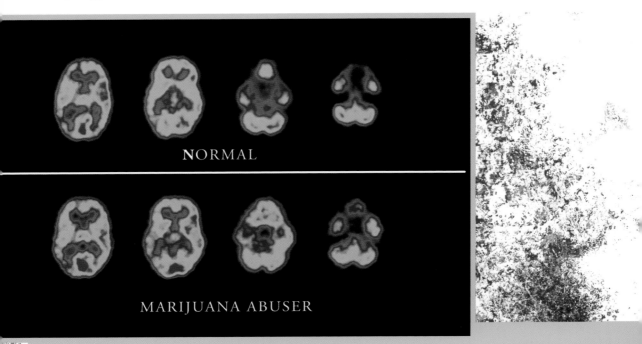

NORMAL

MARIJUANA ABUSER

Scans like these show that marijuana affects the parts of your brain that control coordination, learning, and other important functions.

Marijuana contains cannabinoid chemicals that are not produced by your brain but act as though they are, once they are introduced into the bloodstream. Take THC, for instance. When you smoke pot, THC enters your bloodstream and floods your brain. Once there, it imitates the natural anandamide in your brain and connects with the same receptors. When this happens, your brain releases dopamine or other pleasure neurotransmitters, causing a strong feeling of happiness called euphoria. This is what is known as "getting high."

How Do People Take This Disgusting Drug?

To get high, a person needs to ingest, or take in, the THC in the marijuana plant. This can be done in different ways, including eating it and drinking it as a tea. But by far the most popular form of marijuana use is smoking it.

The leaves and stems of the cannabis plant are lit and turned into vapor, which is taken into and absorbed by the lungs. Marijuana can be rolled up and smoked like a cigarette, or smoked through a pipe or a special water pipe known as a bong. Sometimes, marijuana smokers empty the tobacco out of a cigar and refill the wrapper with pot. This marijuana cigar is called a blunt.

Another form of marijuana is hashish, or hash. Hashish is made from resin, the dark, sticky fluid that is produced by the flowering tops of marijuana plants. This juice is dried and formed into balls or sheets. Users either smoke chunks of hashish or put it in baked goods and eat it. Hashish smoke is usually more potent—and therefore more dangerous— than the smoke produced by dried marijuana leaves.

THC and Your Brain

Whether the marijuana is eaten, drunk, or smoked, the THC in the plant makes its way into your bloodstream and travels to your brain. You never really know how much THC you have ingested and how you will react to

Hashish is a product of the marijuana plant. Like marijuana leaves and buds, chunks of hashish are smoked or eaten.

its effects. Inhalation, or breathing in smoke or vapors, causes effects to come about faster than other ways of ingestion. That's why more users smoke marijuana than take it in other ways. Eating or drinking marijuana puts less concentrated levels of THC into your system. However, the effects you get from ingesting marijuana in cookies, brownies, or tea tend to stick around longer than the effects from smoking the drug. THC starts working soon after it enters your system, usually within minutes. The effects increase in intensity and can last for hours afterward.

The brain is not the only part of your body that absorbs the chemicals in marijuana. Tissues, organs, and especially the fat throughout a person's body can absorb THC, too. The body realizes that the chemical shouldn't be in these places and works to get rid of it. Drugs typically leave your system in urine. This process may take some time, though. Traces of the chemical can stay in your body for quite a while, up to a month or so.

The Trouble with Marijuana

What's wrong with feeling good for a couple of hours? After all, your mind naturally produces a similar chemical, so how can marijuana be bad?

Well, first of all, feeling good isn't the only reaction that your brain can have to THC. After the initial euphoria, users tend to get sleepy and lethargic, which is being lazy to the point of doing absolutely nothing. Other effects may include a lowered body temperature, a heightened sensory awareness (colors and sounds seem more intense), and altered perceptions (things aren't as they seem). Users also have been known to become depressed, or sad, and many also report feeling paranoid. This means they think everyone is making fun of them or is out to get them. Paranoia is a far cry from euphoria.

If you still think marijuana might not be so bad, keep in mind that THC changes the natural order of your brain. In fact, marijuana and THC can mess up your mind so much that it has trouble working normally.

2
Effects
on the Brain

Believe it or not, there are millions of people around the world who choose to damage their brains, some on a daily basis. That's right—marijuana smokers wreck their minds on purpose. Most think they're just changing things on a temporary basis when they get high. Unfortunately, that's not really what happens. Scientists have proven that smoking pot can cause serious damage to your brain. What's worse, the more you smoke, the greater the negative consequences you suffer.

Memory Loss

Pot does a number on your memory. People who use marijuana don't just forget things now and then, like everyone does. When high, they can get lost in the middle of a sentence, unable to remember what they were talking about or just about to say. Problems with memory tend to be the strongest while you are smoking

Smoking pot can leave you extremely confused and forgetful. These side effects may last a long time and get worse the more you smoke.

and for the hours immediately afterward, when you can still feel the effects of marijuana.

Experiments have shown that people who smoke marijuana have memory loss because the chemical THC changes the way neurons communicate in the hippocampus, the section of the brain where memory is stored. To make your memory function normally, brain cells in the hippocampus send messages all at once, what scientists call "in sync." Being in sync gives the brain more power to recall information.

When THC is present in the brain, the cells fire off the same number of memory messages as they normally would, but they don't do it in sync. Apparently, THC attaches itself to receptors on the surface of nerve cells, blocking the steady flow of messages and causing them to become out of sync. Researchers estimate that this can cut a person's ability to remember by about half!

Rats given THC can't remember how to get through a maze they've already figured out. Scientists have shown that the chemicals in pot drastically affect human memory, too.

Smoking marijuana regularly makes neurons age faster than they normally would. This, too, leads to memory loss. As hippocampus neurons get older, they get weaker. That's why people find it hard to remember things as they age. Experiments have shown that laboratory rats that were given THC every day for eight months remembered things more like rats twice their age.

Short-Term vs. Long-Term Memory Problems

Pot smokers almost always have trouble remembering things. Research studies have proven this to be fact. Most of the time, only short-term memory is affected. Short-term memory involves storing small amounts of information for a short amount of time—as little as thirty seconds. Usually, short-term memory troubles get better about a month or so after the person stops smoking pot. However, people who are heavy users of marijuana can experience memory loss for a lot longer. Remember that the more you smoke, the greater the damage.

The news is even worse for young marijuana users. In 2003, researchers from Harvard Medical School and the National Institute on Drug Abuse studied the link between marijuana use and memory. They discovered that people who started smoking pot before they were seventeen years old suffered more long-term memory loss. Scientists think this is because your brain keeps growing until you are in your early twenties. Developing minds are more fragile and open to the effects of drugs. Brain cells that aren't fully formed in teenagers and preteens aren't strong enough to bounce back from the damage done by the chemicals in marijuana. Therefore, the damage done to their memories is worse and longer lasting.

Blood Flow

Cells aren't the only parts of the brain that are in jeopardy when you smoke marijuana. The arteries that carry blood to your brain come under

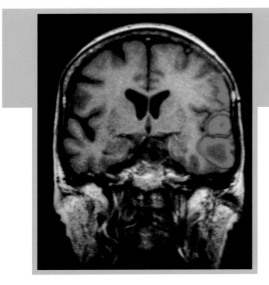

This scan shows part of a brain damaged by a stroke *(in red)*. Damage caused by marijuana use is similar to that caused by a stroke.

attack as well. In order to function properly, your brain needs a steady supply of oxygen, which is carried in the bloodstream. Without oxygen, brain cells start to die. Marijuana smokers have a problem getting enough blood to their brains. It seems that the vessels in a user's brain become too narrow, therefore creating resistance. Increased resistance means less blood gets through to the brain's smaller arteries. As a result, the parts of the brain that control memory and decision-making don't get enough blood and oxygen. The damage this causes is similar to what doctors see in patients with strokes and diabetes.

There is more bad news, according to researchers. The blood flow of those who are heavy marijuana smokers doesn't return to normal even after an entire month of not smoking pot.

Learning and Cognitive Function

Using marijuana makes you stupid. This is not just an expression that describes how you act when you're high. Smoking pot clouds your

Marijuana **and Mental Illness**

An Australian study found that teens who smoked marijuana at least once a week were twice as likely as less frequent users to suffer from depression in later years. Depression is a serious illness that involves the body, mood, and thoughts. It affects the way you eat and sleep, the way you feel about yourself, and the way you think about life in general.

Heavy marijuana smoking has been known to cause anxiety and panic attacks, or intense and sudden feelings of fear.

Schizophrenia is a disabling mental disorder that causes people to disconnect with reality. Smoking pot does not cause schizophrenia, but studies indicate that using marijuana increases the risk of this psychiatric disorder by about 30 percent. In those who have been diagnosed with schizophrenia, using marijuana makes symptoms worse.

mind, making it difficult to pay attention and concentrate. If you can't concentrate, then you can't learn.

More than ruining your concentration, though, marijuana robs you of actual brainpower, or cognitive functioning. This is your ability to know something or figure it out using reason. Many scientific studies show that pot users don't process information as well as nonusers. Need proof? Check out these results of a study published in the scientific journal

Neuroscience. Researchers asked people who regularly smoked marijuana and those who didn't smoke very often to solve problems and make decisions. Those who had rarely smoked pot made mistakes only 8 percent of the time. Long-term smokers, on the other hand, had trouble coming up with answers and made bad decisions 70 percent of the time!

Hallucinations

Hallucinations are a major sign that a person is mentally ill. Hallucination occurs when your senses get twisted. You see, hear, taste, smell, or physically feel things that aren't really there. It's like imagination, but what you sense is incredibly real—to you, anyway. Hallucinations can be weird, such as seeing strange shapes and colors, or they can be creepy, such as feeling like bugs are crawling all over your skin.

Hallucinations caused by using marijuana can be scary. They make it so you can't trust your senses, and you may feel like you're losing your mind.

You may already know that such drugs as LSD and ecstasy can bring about hallucinations. But so can marijuana. This is especially true if a lot of the drug is used at one time, or if the pot has a high THC content. Marijuana is selectively grown to have a high THC content. This makes it more powerful. As a result, more people will want to buy it. Tests conducted by the U.S. government show that the level of THC in commercial pot today is much higher than in the 1970s—anywhere from five times to twenty-five times stronger. Other people say that isn't true. But even if it's not, the fact remains that there are various strengths of pot out there, and you never know the strength of the marijuana until you have smoked it and felt its effects. Increased strength means an increased chance of hallucinating.

The way in which people use marijuana can raise the risk that they will hallucinate. Blunts are cigars hollowed out and filled with pot that's sometimes laced with extra chemicals. The extra ingredient is usually something like PCP or heroin, which are known hallucinogens.

3
Effects
on the Body

As we have seen, many people use marijuana for the so-called pleasurable effect it has on their minds. But they often don't stop to consider what smoking the drug does to their bodies. Let's start with some of the most obvious drawbacks to using marijuana. Smoking pot has the same disgusting side effects that smoking cigarettes has. Your mouth gets dry, which makes tasting, chewing, and speaking harder to do. Your throat gets dry, raw, sore, and itchy, so swallowing becomes difficult. Fumes drift up into your eyes and dry them out, too, giving you a horrible, red, bloodshot look. Your eyes usually look puffy and glassy, too. Finally, smoking leaves behind all sorts of substances that rot away your teeth and gums.

But that's not all. In addition to THC, there are hundreds of other chemicals in pot smoke, and many of them are harmful. These chemicals are often toxic, or act as a poison, to the lungs, heart, nervous system, and other areas of the body.

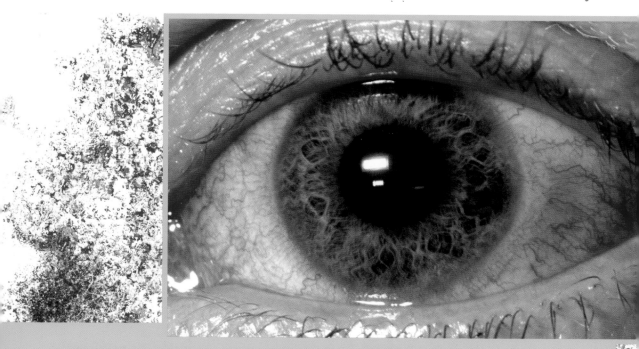

Ugly, bloodshot eyes are typical when you smoke pot. In addition to developing gross red veins, your eyes get swollen and often painfully dry.

Your Respiratory Tract

The respiratory tract is made up of the parts of your body involved with breathing. These include your sinuses, nose, throat, larynx, voice box, and lungs. Normally, you take in air that contains oxygen, which your body needs to keep functioning. Healthy lungs are made of stretchy tissue. They trade oxygen for carbon dioxide, which is a gaseous waste product produced by your cells. Oxygen-rich air flows into your lungs and through alveoli, which are tiny air sacs. This is where the switch of carbon dioxide for oxygen takes place. The alveoli are like filters that trap the good stuff your body needs (oxygen) and push out the stuff it can't use (carbon dioxide).

Marijuana and Your Lungs

Your lungs take the brunt of marijuana's damage to the respiratory tract. Marijuana smoke is considered an irritant because it irritates, or "roughs up," sections of your respiratory tract. In your lungs, particles from smoke attach themselves to the alveoli, clogging them and making it harder for the exchange of carbon dioxide for oxygen to take place. Your body ends up with less oxygen than it needs.

Your lungs react to all this by producing a ton of mucus or phlegm, a gooey substance that sticks to irritants in your system. Your body gets rid of phlegm by having it run out of your nose or, in the case of smoking, coughing it up to force it out of your lungs. As a result of having a lot of phlegm, you wheeze and struggle to breathe. You also develop what's known as "smoker's cough." Smokers tend to cough up tar resin and other awful chemicals, which make the phlegm they produce a gross brown color. Other times, you might cough up phlegm that is green or yellow, which means there's some kind of infection in your lungs. Doesn't that sound pretty?

You don't need to be a heavy marijuana smoker for this to happen. The equivalent of one joint a day is all it takes.

Over time, marijuana smoke can turn a healthy lung, like the one on the left above, into a shriveled and pretty much useless organ.

Emphysema

When the lungs are under attack from smoke, they release substances that fight the invading toxins. Unfortunately, these same substances can attack the healthy tissue of the lungs. Eventually, a smoker's lung tissue may lose its flexibility and the bronchial tubes collapse, trapping air in the alveoli and making them expand and burst. This condition is called emphysema.

Worse than Smoking Cigarettes

You probably know about the terrible damage that smoking cigarettes can do to you. Some scientists think smoking marijuana is even more harmful than smoking cigarettes. One reason is that pot users hold smoke in their lungs for as long as possible in order to get a stronger high. Therefore, the smoke is in contact with lung tissues for longer periods and ends up doing more damage.

Because it rots away your gums and makes your teeth yellow, smoking—marijuana or cigarettes—totally ruins your smile. More than that, an unhealthy mouth can lead to more serious illness.

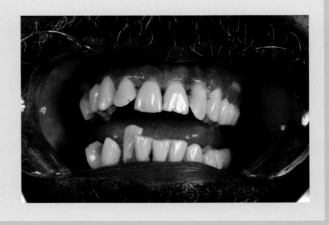

Emphysema is the most common cause of death from respiratory disease in the United States, and it is the fourth-most-common cause of death overall. In addition to smoker's cough, emphysema causes shortness of breath, weight loss, headaches, and chronic fatigue. In later stages, it puts you at risk for pulmonary hypertension, a life-threatening disease affecting the arteries that supply the lungs with blood. Severe emphysema leads to respiratory failure, a condition in which the lungs no longer exchange carbon dioxide for oxygen. There is no cure for emphysema.

Bronchitis and Pneumonia

Smoking marijuana makes the lungs more susceptible to bronchitis and pneumonia. Bronchitis affects the bronchial tubes, which are the air's passageways to the lungs. The inner walls of the tubes swell and become narrow, reducing their ability to take in air. Pneumonia is an infection that affects the lung tissue, filling it with pus and mucus. Symptoms of these diseases include a hacking cough, fever and chills, a burning ache, tightness in the chest, wheezing or "rattling" in the lungs, and fatigue.

Your Heart

From the first puff you take until hours later, when the high starts to wear off, marijuana makes your heart beat faster. According to most studies, the heart may beat anywhere from 20 to 100 percent faster. The rate at which blood is pumped throughout the body also rises when pot smoke enters the system. Once the heart gets racing, a lot of things can happen.

Marijuana and Cancer

So far, researchers have been unable to establish a definitive link between marijuana use and cancer. However, this does not mean that marijuana smoke definitely does not cause cancer. Scientists simply haven't been able to prove any connection. Consider that:

- Tar is a harmful resin produced by burning plants. One marijuana joint has the same amount of tar as four cigarettes.
- The tar in marijuana smoke is high in carcinogens, the chemicals that cause cancer.
- Studies show that smoking pot may increase your risk of developing head, neck, and lung cancer. This is especially true for people who smoke both tobacco and marijuana.

First of all, a racing heartbeat causes discomfort. You could get terribly dizzy and pass out, or you might have trouble breathing. In the worst case, if you already have a pre-existing heart condition, you could suffer a heart attack.

Doctors and researchers aren't sure if it's inhaling the THC, carbon monoxide, bits of burnt leaf, or some combination of substances in marijuana smoke that causes these reactions. All they know is that they are real, and marijuana should be considered a danger to the heart.

Your Reproductive System

Something marijuana users may not even be aware of is that smoking pot can affect your reproductive system. It can change the level of sex hormones, affect your sexual development, and even determine whether or not you can have a baby.

The body may store THC in the tissues of the sex organs. Experts believe that the buildup of this psychoactive chemical influences the level of hormones in regular marijuana users, both men and women. In women, THC affects the sex hormones estrogen and progesterone, causing irregular menstrual cycles. In men, it lowers the level of testosterone, which reduces their sperm count. Irregular menstrual cycles and a low sperm count are common reasons for infertility, or why a couple would be unable to have a baby.

Even if a man has a normal sperm count, fertility problems can still occur because of THC in marijuana. Normally, sperm start to swim very fast when they get close to a woman's egg. This is called hyperactivation. When exposed to THC, sperm start the hyperactivation process right away, and they basically tire themselves out before they can reach the egg. If the sperm don't reach and fertilize the egg, pregnancy cannot happen. In short, if you plan on having children, it would be smart to stay away from marijuana.

4
Nasty
Behavior

By now you have an idea of what using marijuana can do to your mind and your body. Now let's take a look at what pot can do to your behavior. Any psychoactive (mind-altering) substance like THC is going to influence how you act and react. It can and does change your mood and coordination. Usually pot's effects are temporary, but obviously they happen every time you use the drug. Eventually, with regular use, how you act while high becomes the new normal for you. In other words, marijuana changes not only your perception of the world, but also how the world perceives you.

Studies conducted over several years have shown that teenagers and preteens who use marijuana tend to develop behavioral issues. They don't achieve—in school or in life—nearly as well as people the same age who abstain, or decide not to do drugs. Marijuana users are more likely to get in trouble and hang out with people who also are delinquent.

You put your safety and even your life on the line when you smoke marijuana. Pot affects your judgment and reflexes, making accidents more likely to happen.

Lack of Judgment

Using marijuana clouds your thinking. That's because when you consume pot, your brain is flooded with THC. Often, your mind is so busy enjoying the feeling of euphoria that you don't feel the need to consider more practical matters, such as your surroundings, your safety, or the consequences of your actions. Basically, you lack the necessary judgment to make good decisions. Bad judgment frequently leads to risky behavior, or activities that put you in danger. Risky behavior is behavior that you usually will be sorry for later.

Having unprotected sex or getting behind the wheel of a car while high are risky behaviors associated with marijuana use and lack of judgment. According to the National Center on Addiction and Substance Abuse at Columbia University, teen girls who smoked pot are much more likely to get pregnant than those who do not use marijuana. Likewise, teen boys who smoked pot are much more likely to get a girl pregnant than those who do not use.

As for driving, a study conducted by the U.S. National Highway Traffic Safety Administration showed that a person's ability to drive safely was impaired by even a relatively small dose of marijuana. Subjects of the study performed poorly when it came to reaction time and adjusting speed to go along with the flow of traffic. They also were less aware of their surroundings, including other cars in the area. Drivers are much more dangerous to themselves and others when they lack these safe driving skills.

Not using good judgment puts you at greater risk for accidents and injury. The use of illegal drugs, including marijuana, is a reason why many people wind up in the emergency rooms of American hospitals each year. The Substance Abuse and Mental Health Services Administration (SAMHSA) keeps track of all sorts of information related to drug use. According to a report issued by SAMHSA in 2007, the number of injuries caused at least in part by marijuana use has risen in recent years. In 2001, for example, marijuana was responsible for about 110,000 emergency room visits in the United States. By 2005, the figure had more than doubled, to 242,200 visits.

Lethargy

A big reason why most people use marijuana is that it slows things down and relaxes them. The problem is that regular use can relax you a little too much. The high you get from pot is typically followed by sleepiness and a "Who cares?" attitude. This leads to lethargy, which is a total lack of motivation to do anything, even the things you used to care about a great deal.

Getting high all the time is especially harmful when you are young. You lose the motivation to do and learn about new and exciting things.

Long-term pot users may suffer from what scientists call "amotivational syndrome." This means they become moody and depressed, in addition to not being motivated. Users themselves have a word to describe the state of being totally lethargic: "burnout." Pot smokers who experience burnout move slowly and can't pay attention to anything or anyone. Sometimes, they are not even aware of where they are and what is going on around them. The truly scary thing is that they act like this all the time, not just right after they've been smoking.

Other Behavioral Issues

Using marijuana might make you think that you are pleasant to be around because the high makes you so mellow. However, there are other behavioral issues that can make people want to avoid you. For instance, personal hygiene can be a big problem for marijuana users. When you use pot,

The chemicals in pot make your body crave more food than it needs. The result is binge eating, which can make you grossly overweight.

your eyes get red and glassy and your teeth get brown. In addition to always having the stink of pot smoke on their clothes and in their hair, users may let their appearance and even their health go because they are so lethargic. In the end, smoking pot can cause the people you care about—your friends and family members—to avoid your company.

Then there is the increased appetite that comes with smoking marijuana. This potentially disgusting urge is known as "the munchies." Recent studies of brain chemistry indicate that THC and other cannabinoids stimulate the glands that tell the brain that the body needs nourishment. They also may disable the neurons that tell your brain your stomach is full and to stop eating. As a result, pot smokers tend to eat a lot when they are high. The real problem is that they tend to indulge in salty or sugary snacks, rather than healthful foods such as fruits and vegetables. Having the munchies causes pot smokers to gain weight, which, over time, can ruin their health. Couple that with the fact that regular marijuana users tend to be tired all the time and lack the motivation to exercise, and you have users who are overweight and sickly.

Finally, those who often use marijuana risk being labeled a "stoner." You might not think this is such a big deal, but it could be. Once you are pegged as a drug user, you can develop a bad reputation among teachers and coaches at your school, employers, police officers, and other authority figures.

Addiction

Perhaps the worst behavior that can result from marijuana use is becoming a pot addict. Addiction occurs when you feel normal only when you take a certain substance regularly. Here's how it works:

The unnatural substances found in drugs trick your brain into believing it is getting normal amounts of natural chemicals. But these amounts are not normal. When you take drugs, you add extra chemicals to the ones that your brain already makes. It's as if you are giving it too much to handle. Your brain tries to adjust to these higher levels by reducing the amount of chemicals that it naturally produces. As a result, the level of natural chemicals is too low. You wind up having to smoke pot to get your chemical levels up and your brain back on track.

When you need a drug in order to feel normal, you are dependent on that drug. There are two kinds of drug dependence: physical and psychological. When you are physically addicted to a drug, it changes your mind and body so much that you actually must have the substance to function properly. Psychological addiction to a substance is different. It occurs when your mind is convinced that you have to keep using, even though your body would be able to function without it.

Is Marijuana Addictive?

There is a huge debate about whether a person can be addicted to marijuana. Some say yes, and some say users can stop at any time and not feel any ill effects. Others say pot is only psychologically addictive and that smoking pot is merely something that users do out of habit.

When you're addicted to a drug, you run the risk of going through withdrawal. This is the physical and mental sickness that an addicted person goes through when he or she stops taking drugs. Studies have shown that longtime marijuana users experience withdrawal symptoms when they stop using the drug. These symptoms include anxiousness and increased irritability. Withdrawal symptoms with marijuana are not as strong as they are with other drugs such as cocaine or heroin, but they are still felt by the user.

In addition to causing withdrawal, marijuana meets other criteria that doctors and scientists use to say whether a drug is addictive:

- **Intoxication**—the substance is able to intoxicate you, or get you high
- **Reinforcement**—the substance provides such a good feeling, it makes you want to keep taking it
- **Tolerance**—the more you take the substance, the more your body and mind get used to it, so you have to take more to satisfy your need for it
- **Dependence**—you have a tough time quitting, or are unable to quit taking, the substance; you depend on it to make you feel normal

Using these points as a guide, experts have determined that marijuana is at least mildly addictive. Because of people's genetic differences, the addiction may be stronger in some users than it is for others.

Professionals in the field of substance abuse look at additional factors to judge whether or not a person is addicted to a drug. For instance, they want to know if the user spends a lot of time trying to get the drug or thinking about getting high. Being willing to give up other things—friendships, favorite activities, your health, and your future—just to get high is another sign of addiction. If a person seems to use a drug all the time, or gets high at school, at work, or while driving, then he or

Group counseling can help recovering users stay away from marijuana and avoid the pain of addiction.

she may be addicted. If you keep taking a drug even when it is clear that its use can hurt you, or it already has hurt you, then you are definitely addicted.

The Ultimate Risk

Consider your options regarding marijuana. Because it can be considered an addictive substance, marijuana can, at least to some degree, control you and leave you powerless. On top of that, it wrecks your developing brain and chokes the life out of you by scarring your lungs. If that weren't enough to repulse you, marijuana also can make you look and act like a lazy slob and an idiot. Given the negative effects associated with marijuana, just using the drug is the biggest risk of all.

Glossary

addict One who compulsively uses a substance that is known to be harmful.

alveoli Tiny air sacs in the lungs that exchange carbon dioxide for oxygen.

anandamide Naturally occurring chemical that works in the brain like THC, the active ingredient in marijuana.

bong Type of water pipe used to smoke marijuana.

cannabinoid Receptor neuron in the brain that is especially sensitive to the chemicals found in cannabis (marijuana).

cognitive Related to the ability to know something or figure it out using reason.

compromise To impair or weaken.

dependence State of being unable to function normally without something, in this case, the chemicals in marijuana.

hallucinate To see, hear, touch, smell, or taste something that seems real but isn't actually there.

hemp Common name of the plant family to which marijuana belongs.

hippocampus Area of the brain that controls memory.

hygiene Practice of taking care of your physical appearance and your health.

intoxication Drunkenness or state of being high.

lethargy Lack of motivation, energy, or caring about anything.

munchies Greatly increased appetite brought about by using marijuana.

neurons Nerve cells; brain neurons oversee all the activity in your brain.

neurotransmitter Chemicals produced by your brain that let neurons communicate with one another.

perception Way in which you are aware of and understand something.

psychoactive Able to change your mood and the way you think.

respiratory tract Parts of your body that have to do with breathing.

THC (delta-9-tetrahydrocannabinol) Psychoactive chemical in marijuana that makes you high.

tolerance Capacity of the body to withstand intoxicants. Having a high tolerance requires increasing amounts of a substance for a person just to feel normal.

toxic Extremely harmful.

withdrawal Physical and mental sickness an addicted person goes through when he or she stops taking drugs.

Canadian Centre on Substance Abuse

75 Albert Street, Suite 300

Ottawa, ON K1P 5E7

Canada

(613) 235-4048

Web site: http://www.ccsa.ca/CCSA/EN/TopNav/Home

The Canadian Centre on Substance Abuse (CCSA) provides national leadership, analysis, and advice to reduce alcohol- and other drug-related harms.

National Clearinghouse for Alcohol & Drug Information

P.O. Box 2345

Rockville, MD 20847-2345

(800) 729-6686

Web site: http://ncadi.samhsa.gov

SAMHSA's National Clearinghouse for Alcohol and Drug Information (NCADI) is a resource for information about substance abuse prevention and addiction treatment.

National Institute on Drug Abuse (NIDA)

National Institutes of Health (NIH)

6001 Executive Boulevard, Room 5213

Bethesda, MD 20892-9561

Web sites: http://www.nida.nih.gov; http://www.drugabuse.gov

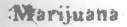

NIDA's mission is to lead the United States in bringing the power of science to bear on drug abuse and addiction.

Partnership for a Drug-Free America

405 Lexington Avenue, Suite 1601

New York, NY 10174

(212) 922-1560

Web site: http://www.drugfree.org

The mission of the nonprofit Partnership for a Drug-Free America is to reduce illicit drug use in America.

White House Office on National Drug Control Policy

Drug Policy Information Clearinghouse

P.O. Box 6000

Rockville, MD 20849

(800) 666-3332

Web site: http://www.whitehousedrugpolicy.gov

The principal purpose of ONDCP is to establish policies, priorities, and objectives for the United States government drug control program.

Web Sites

Due to the changing nature of Internet links, Rosen Publishing has developed an online list of Web sites related to the subject of this book. This site is updated regularly. Please use this link to access the list:

http://www.rosenlinks.com/idd/mari

For Further Reading

Bingham, Jane. *Marijuana: What's the Deal?* Port Melbourne, Australia: Heineman, 2005.

Carroll, Jamuna, ed. *Opposing Viewpoints: Marijuana*. Chicago, IL: Greenhaven Press, 2005.

Daly, Melissa, Francois Jaud, and Pierre Mezinski. *Drugs Explained: The Real Deal on Alcohol, Pot, Ecstasy, and More.* New York, NY: Sunscreen/Reed Business Information, 2004.

Keyishan, Elizabeth. *Everything You Need to Know About Smoking*. New York, NY: Rosen Publishing Group, 2003.

Leonard-Brown, Sarah. *Marijuana* (Health Issues). Orlando, FL: Raintree, 2004.

Marcovitz, Hal. *Marijuana*. Chicago, IL: Lucent Books, 2006.

McMullen, Janet. *The History of Drugs—Marijuana*. Chicago, IL: Greenhaven Press, 2004.

Melhing, Randi, and David Triggle. *Marijuana* (Drugs: The Straight Facts). New York, NY: Chelsea House Publishers, 2003.

Rees, Jonathan. *Drugs* (It's Your Health). North Mankato, MN: Smart Apple Media, 2005.

Stanley, Debbie. *Marijuana and Your Lungs: The Incredibly Disgusting Story*. New York, NY: Rosen Publishing Group, 2000.

Bibliography

American Council for Drug Education. "Basic Facts About Drugs: Marijuana." Retrieved July 6, 2007 (http://www.acde.org/common/Marijana.htm).

Arizona Industrial Hemp Council. "Hemp vs. Marijuana." 2001. Retrieved June 29, 2007 (http://azhemp.org/Archive/Package/Legal/legal.html).

Bell, Ryan, Paul Beitsayad, and Sarah Bogen. "Marijuana Use: The Hard Facts." *La Voz*, February 21, 2006, p. 11.

Ben-Joseph, Elana Pearl, and Stephen Eppes, eds. "Pneumonia." October 2006. Retrieved July 5, 2007 (http://kidshealth.org/teen/infections/bacterial_viral/pneumonia.html).

Bonsor, Kevin. HowStuffWorks. "How Marijuana Works." July 2, 2001. Retrieved June 30, 2007 (http://health.howstuffworks.com/marijuana3.htm).

Britt, Robert Roy. "Up In Smoke: Marijuana Toasts Memory." March 13, 2006. Retrieved July 1, 2007 (http://www.livescience.com/health/060313_pot_brain.html).

Chudler, Eric H. "Neuroscience for Kids: Marijuana." Retrieved June 28, 2007 (http://faculty.washington.edu/chudler/mari.html).

DeNoon, Daniel J. WebMD. "Smoking Marijuana Lowers Fertility." October 13, 2003. Retrieved July 6, 2007 (http://men.webmd.com/news/20031013/smoking-marijuana-lowers-fertility).

Drug Policy Alliance. "Marijuana: The Facts—Medical Marijuana." April 10, 2006. Retrieved July 9, 2007 (http://www.drugpolicy.org/marijuana/medical).

Eisner, Robin. "Marijuana Abuse: Age of Initiation, Pleasure of Response Foreshadow Young Adult Outcomes." January 2005.

Retrieved July 1, 2007 (http://www.drugabuse.gov/NIDA_notes/NNvol19N5/ Marijuana.html).

Gorski, Terrence T. "Special Report on Marijuana: Part Two, Effects of Marijuana." October 14, 2002. Retrieved July 1, 2007 (http://www.tgorski.com/drug_ updates/Marijuana/Marijuana_02_021014.htm).

Herning, Ronald I., et. al. "Cerebrovascular Perfusion in Marijuana Users During a Month of Monitored Abstinence." *Neurology*, Vol. 64, February 2005, pp. 404–405.

Hilts, Philip J. "Is Nicotine Addictive? It Depends on Whose Criteria You Use." *New York Times*, August 2, 1994.

Khamsi, Roxanne. "Marijuana Wrecks Havoc on Brain's Memory Cells." November 2006. Retrieved July 1, 2007 (http://www.newscientist.com/ channel/health/dn10607-marijuana-wreaks-havoc-on-brains-memory-cells.html).

Macintosh, Sara. "Pot and Personality: Memory, Motivation and Behavior." February 2007. Retrieved July 7, 2007 (http://www.doitnow.org/pdfs/125.pdf).

Marijuana Research Today. "Information About Marijuana." Retrieved July 1, 2007 (http://marijuana.researchtoday.net/about-marijuana.htm).

McDougal, Jeanette. "Cannabis Hemp THC in the Food-Cosmetic Supply." August 2000. Retrieved June 29, 2007 (http://www.drugwatch.org/Cannabis% 20Hemp%20THC.htm).

Messinis, Lambros, et. al. "Neuropsychological Deficits in Long-Term Frequent Cannabis Users." *Neurology*, Vol. 66, Issue 5, March 2006, p. 737.

Nagle, Jeanne. *Everything You Need to Know About Drug Addiction*. New York, NY: Rosen Publishing Group, 1999.

Narconon of Southern California. "FAQ About Marijuana." Retrieved July 6, 2007 (http://www.addictionca.com/FAQ-marijuana.htm).

National Institute on Drug Abuse. "Research Report Series—Marijuana Abuse." July 1, 2005. Retrieved July 3, 2007 (http://www.nida.nih.gov/ ResearchReports/Marijuana/Marijuana3.html).

New Scientist. "Pot-Smoking Your Way to Memory Loss." March 18, 2006. Retrieved July 1, 2007 (http://www.newscientist.com/channel/health/mg18925434.900.htm)

Office of National Drug Control Policy. "What Americans Need to Know About Marijuana." October 2003. Retrieved July 7, 2007 (http://www.whitehouse-drugpolicy.gov/publications/amer_know_marij/myths.pdf).

Publishers Group, LLC. "Hashish." 2006. Retrieved June 29, 2007 (http://www.streetdrugs.org/hashish.htm).

Substance Abuse and Mental Health Services Administration. "Emergency Room Visits Climb for Misuse of Prescription and Over-the-Counter Drugs." March 13, 2007. Retrieved July 7, 2007 (http://www.samhsa.gov/newsroom/advisories/0703135521.aspx).

Substance Abuse and Mental Health Services Administration. "Marijuana Potency Has Increased Over Time." Retrieved July 1, 2007 (http://family.samhsa.gov/set/marijuana.aspx).

Swartout-Corbeil, Deanne M. "Look Smart: Emphysema." Retrieved July 1, 2007 (http://findarticles.com/p/articles/mi_gGENH/is_/ai_2699003270).

Tashkin, Donald M.D. "Effects of Marijuana on the Lungs and Its Immune Defenses." March 1997. Retrieved July 4, 2007 (http://ukcia.org/research/EffectsOfMarijuanaOnLungAndImmuneDefenses.html).

University of Pittsburgh Student Health Service. "Health Education: Marijuana." July 20, 2001. Retrieved July 6, 2007 (http://www.pitt.edu/~studhlth/studenthealthed_wbpage/Alcohol/links/page9marijuana.html).

Wysong, Pippa. "Marijuana Use Can Lead to Blood Flow Problems in the Brain." April 5, 2005. Retrieved July 2, 2007 (http://www.accessexcellence.org/WN/SU/dopebrainap05.htm).

Index

About the Author

Jeanne Nagle is a journalist and writer based in Rochester, N.Y. She has researched and written extensively on the effects of drugs on children and young adults. Her works include *Drug Addiction* and *Polysubstance Abuse.*

Photo Credits

Cover, p. 1 © www.istockphoto.com/Jordan Phillips; p. 3 © www.istockphoto.com/ Oliver Ingrouille; p. 7 © www.istockphoto.com/Shaun Lombard; © Pascal Goetgheluck/ Science Photo Library/Custom Medical Stock Photo; p. 12 DEA; p. 15 © www. istockphoto.com; p. 16 © Will & Demi McIntyre/Photo Researchers; p. 18 © Scott Camazine/Photo Researchers; © A. Wilson/Custom Medical Stock Photo; p. 23 © Dr. P. Marazzi/Photo Researchers; p. 25 © Arthur Glauberman/Photo Researchers; p. 27 © Custom Medical Stock Photo; p. 31 © www.istockphoto.com/Luis Santana; p. 33 © Bob Daemmrich/Photo Edit; p. 34 © Bill Aron/Photo Edit; p. 38 © Mary Kate Denny/Photo Edit.

Designer: Les Kanturek; **Editor:** Christopher Roberts;
Photo Researcher: Marty Levick